I0086156

TAMING THE BEAST

How to Stop Panic & Start Peace

REBELL R. WADE

All rights reserved.

No part of this publication may be reproduced or transmitted in any form or by any means, mechanical or electronic, including photocopying and recording, or by any information storage or retrieval system, without permission in writing from author or publisher (except by a reviewer, who may quote brief passages and/or show brief video clips in a review.

CONTENTS

INTRODUCTION

〰〰〰

*H*ello, my name is Rebell and I am a recovered agoraphobic. That wasn't how you were expecting me to finish that sentence, was it? But that ending is no less dramatic or life damaging than if I would have said alcoholic or addict.

Agoraphobia can make you feel just as out of control as being an alcoholic or addict can. For several years, I was afraid to leave my own home. When I did have to venture out, I went with my safe person and even then, I was terrified of being in a place I couldn't get out of. Drive-thru lines for banks or fast-food restaurants became worse for me than any boogeyman.

Ask any alcoholic and they can usually tell you not only when they had their first drink, but also how it made them feel. The same goes for an agoraphobic. You become agoraphobic when anxiety, anxiety attacks, and/or panic attacks have become so bad that you have developed an extreme or irrational fear of entering open or crowded places. You become afraid to leave your own home or of being in a place from which you can't escape.

I can remember that first anxiety attack way back in fourth grade that eventually led to me being home bound. This is far from a fun way to live. In fact, it's miserable. It's a place

I don't want you to ever be. It is a place I wouldn't have been if I had learned about anxiety and what was going on inside of me. I just knew that I had this monster that was battling me for control and winning. I hated this monster, and hate is a strong word that I rarely use. This monster would show up unexpectedly and take over my world. This monster was terrifying!

Everyone is born with this monster inside of them. It is a monster that once its ugly head is reared, will change your life. However, it is a monster we must tame to be able to live the life we want. This monster is anxiety and do not kid yourself, it can feel like it is going to eat you alive, as much as coming face to face with a saber tooth tiger coming off a week-long diet.

Notice I said that everyone is born with this inside of them, yet strangely, for some, this monster will never make itself known. It will never show its ugly, life altering face. Those of us with it often look at those who don't have it and wonder if they are even from the same planet, but more about these weirdos later. Let's get back to us. Us, as in you and ME.

Wait! Did I say me? Did I admit to having anxiety? Did I really say that I get this terrible, horrible, icky-bad feeling? You bet I did! Why the drama here? Because when we are feeling anxiety, the **last** thing we want to do is admit it or share that we are not feeling "normal". Now in the spirit of transparency, it took me a long time to learn that sharing that I was feeling anxious with someone actually helped my level of anxiety go down.

This is why we are here, you and me. This is why I am taking the time to write this, and you are taking the time to read it. I learned how to not only make the symptoms decrease, but to disappear.

This is the reason I am putting another self-help book about anxiety on the already overloaded market. Because this book might just be *the one* that resonates with you. This book may be *the one* that makes you feel like you are not alone. My hopes and prayers are that this book *is the* one that encourages you to take control of your monster. and not just to tame it, but to slay it.

I did! The real, bottom-line reason that I am taking the time to write this (because I could be riding my motorcycle) is because I had dealt with anxiety and panic attacks for years before I became agoraphobic. Next, I spent a couple of years living with agoraphobia before I realized that this was a roommate that I would do anything to evict. I do not want it to take you the years it took me to learn to live a rich and full life; one free of anxiety.

If you are tired of the emotional roller coaster of anxiety, and if you are ready to tame this monster and enjoy this big, beautiful world that holds so many possibilities for you, then read on.

Read on knowing that you are not the first to go through this, and you certainly will not be the last.

Read on knowing that you are not alone!

Read on knowing that this is my story. It is how I tamed the monster living inside of me. It is what worked for me and has been working for decades.

Hugs……

CHAPTER 1

A MONSTER IS BORN

◇◇◇

(Disclaimer: I am not a doctor and I have never played one on TV. I am not writing this from a doctor's standpoint. I am writing this from my standpoint. It is my story. It is how I see anxiety; it is about my experiences with anxiety. Mostly, it is how I helped improve my anxiety. This book is about what worked for me and has been working for decades.)

*A*nxiety is rarely a one and done event. A little anxiety makes us feel bad. It is uncomfortable. Because it makes us feel bad and is uncomfortable, a little anxiety leads to more anxiety. We brace against having it. When we continue to brace against it, it leads us to having an anxious life.

Living an anxious life is horrible! It sucks! It wears you out! It hurts you physically! It hurts you mentally! It hurts your relationships! IT HURTS YOU! Wow, that is a lot of exclamation points. But, if you are reading this, chances are that you are not feeling your best right now because of anxiety and you are probably thinking that putting three or more exclamation points behind each of those statements would be much more accurate.

Anxiety, in one form or another, has disrupted your life and you are ready to do something about it. If anxiety is a mild disruption, you could just not be feeling you. You could have some mild stomach upsets, or maybe you have a little tightness in your chest that lets you know all is not well in your world. If your anxiety is a severe disruption to your day to day life, then your symptoms are making you miserable. They do more than let you know all is not right in your world. These symptoms are shouting at you that your world is about to end, or you are about to experience some catastrophic event. The anxiety, the symptoms, the feelings, the doom, and gloom have a profound effect on you over time. They wear you out, figuratively, and literally. I know this because I lived the exhausting life of anxiety and panic attacks.

My first experience with anxiety happened in the fourth grade. Of course, I didn't know that it was anxiety way back then. I just knew I began feeling strange and I didn't like. I didn't like it enough that I was willing to do whatever it took to not feel that way again.

On the other hand, they could be a serious interrupter to your life, making you want help now. They could have you sweaty and shaking as you reach for the Ativan or Xanax, as you think of ways to get out of doing whatever it is you have to do today or have planned to do today.

At my worst, I was agoraphobic for two years. Yes, you read that right. I didn't leave my home at all unless I was with my safe person, my husband. It was still hard to leave even with him and I limited my trips out to only necessary ones such as going to the grocery store or to doctor's appointments.

I didn't get that way overnight. I didn't have a learning manual, if you will, a book like this to answer my questions and guide me back to a healthy and happy place. If I would have, I would have been able to save myself years of pain, agony, despair, all fathered by anxiety.

That is why I am writing this. It is for you. I want it to be precise and to the point. I don't want you to have to wait for help while or after reading everything on the internet or everything in the bookstore. That help is just too far away. My goal is to help you begin feeling better now, sooner rather than later. There is not a word quota or certain podcast length you have to experience before you get real results.

Let me prove that right now, and in a way that does not benefit me at all. Stop reading this and go to the website www. potentialsunlimited.com. Purchase and download their Relieve Stress & Anxiety recording and begin listening to it. File 1 is a subliminal recording. It is instrumental and the relaxation and stress relieving techniques are hidden in the music. I suggest listening to File 2 first. File 2 is a voice recording and I have used it for over twenty years. It will talk you through a relaxation and then a self-hypnosis, which I have also used for twenty years, to help you relieve your anxiety. I will explain how and why it works later in this book. For right now, this will get you started relieving your anxiety. Again, I get nothing monetarily from that company; no kickbacks, no little something extra in my Christmas stocking, nothing. I just get the satisfaction of helping you.

Back to my anxious life. As I stated earlier, my first experience with anxiety was in the fourth grade. We were sitting in class watching what was intended to be a motivational documentary. It was about a woman who had lost both arms and could do anything with her feet. Our teacher had good intentions. She wanted us to know that we could overcome any obstacle that life threw at us. However, somewhere between her good intentions and watching this amazing woman grocery shop using her feet as hands, I began to imagine how horrible it must be to have everyone stare at you like her fellow shoppers were doing. This thought changed into, what if that happened to me. Suddenly, I was terrified of going through life without arms and having to use my feet as hands. The thought of the curious stares that I would receive sent me spiraling. Now I know that my body tensed, and my breathing became too shallow. As the time, I only knew that I had begun feeling strange. I was dizzy and there was a white halo around everything I looked at.

I stumbled to the teacher's desk and told her that I didn't feel good. She promptly sent me to the nurse and my mother was called. She took me home, fed me lunch and told me to go take a nap. Since I began feeling better once I was out of the classroom and away from the film, not too much was said or done about it. The episode was considered a one and done deal to my parents. For me it opened the "what if" door; what if it happened again? What if it happened again and the school couldn't reach my parents? What if it happened again and the horrible feeling got worse? How much worse could it get? Etc. Etc. Etc.

Months would pass before I had another anxiety episode. Again, I wouldn't recognize it as anxiety until a decade and half later. My next serious episode happened while we were traveling from Texas to Indiana. We were making the sixteen-hour drive from our little town to Purdue University for my father to take a two-week course to become a Welding Inspector. This was back in the day of intricately folded paper road maps and long before seatbelts were mandatory. This was when you could sleep in the back window and let the sun blast you through the glass.

Somewhere around St. Louis, I began to worry about my beloved grandmother being without me for two whole weeks. We were extremely close and I while I was excited to travel, I was anxious about being away from her. As we stopped for the night, I began having severe stomach cramps. To the ER we go, and surprise, surprise, the doctor couldn't find anything wrong with me. He finally decided that it was a slight case of traveler's tummy and carsickness. Liquid pink medicine was administered, back to the hotel room we went where I spent a miserable night.

The following day we made it to Effingham, Indiana, when my mother happened to glance in the back seat. She saw that my hands were turning a bluish-purple color. Alerting my father, they quickly found another ER and we stopped for round 2. I will never forget the doctor on shift. He was from Germany and spoke with a heavy accent. He didn't just examine me physically. He took the time to ask me questions and not just the usual "where does it hurt" ones either. After visiting with me for fifteen or twenty minutes, he left the room only to return shortly with phone. He plugged it into the wall and told me to call my grandmother. I dialed her number on the rotary phone and I can still remember the clicking sound it made and feel the coolness of the metal dial as my finger spun the wheel. She answered and we talked for a bit. When I hung up, he turned to my parents and explained to them that I had started hyperventilating because I wasn't thinking good thoughts. He also told them to let me call my grandmother every day while traveling. This would keep us both healthy, he said with a confident smile. My parents did and the doctor was right. I stayed healthy and we had a great trip. I had no other bouts of stomach cramps or hyperventilation for the rest of the trip.

I wish that I could say that I didn't have any other issues for a long time, but I would be lying. For the next decade and half, I dealt with unexplainable bouts of nausea and vomiting and dizziness. These sometimes landed me in the ER, but the diagnosis was always vague, ranging from a stomach bug to an inner ear disturbance. I never once realized that these bouts only happened when I was stressed or upset. What a difference just knowing this early on would have made on my life.

It took my world collapsing before I began asking why I had these strange bouts of illness.

I was in my mid-twenties, happily married and six months pregnant. We were at the hospital excitedly getting our mid-trimester ultrasound done. Keep in mind that back then they didn't do them as frequently as they do now which made this a much-anticipated day. The technician came in and flipped the machine on with a smile saying, "Let's see what we have here."

The monitor glowed a soft gray and we looked at it excitedly, not at all sure what we were seeing. Other pregnant friends had shared their experiences of seeing the baby move and the heart beating so this is what we were expecting to see. That isn't what we saw at all. We saw stillness. A simple, profound stillness. Both my husband and I knew that this wasn't right. We knew something was wrong. The technician's behavior confirmed it as she turned off the monitor, then quickly stood up and announced that she needed to get the doctor. We didn't say anything as she left, and he entered just mere seconds apart. He sat down at the machine and tapped the button turning it back on. I wanted to ask what was wrong and why wasn't I seeing any movement, but I didn't. I remained silent, as did my husband. I think we both already knew the answers to our unspoken questions. He turned from the screen and his eyes answered us before he even spoke. "Mr. and Mrs. Wade, I am so sorry to tell you this, but your babies have died. It looks like you are carrying a boy and a girl in the same sack and only identical twins can share a sack."

My mind focused on the only acceptable thing he said, then I remember questioning, "Twins?"

"Yes, you are carrying twins. One has passed in the last couple of days and the other one looks to have passed a day or two before that."

His acceptable word quickly became overtaken by his unacceptable ones. My world stopped as all his words sank in. This couldn't be happening. A soft gray began surrounding me as a numbness set in; a numbness that I had never experienced before. A numbness that I now know was a form of denial.

I vaguely remembering them calling my doctor and him telling us to report to the hospital early the next morning so that they could induce labor. We did, and after a fourteen-hour labor, I delivered a perfectly formed boy and girl. They were simply improperly housed inside my body.

The delivery that should have been exciting and filled with wonder, was instead filled with devasting loss and profound sadness.

No one advised us to take our time and deal with our loss. No one told us it was okay to be sad, or angry, or whatever we were feeling.

Instead, everyone said that this was a fluke of nature, a mistake. They told us it wouldn't happen again, and the answer was to try to get pregnant right away.

I wrapped up all the grief, all the anger, all the denial, all the numbness, and all the fear and shoved it down deep inside and focused on getting pregnant again. It was the early nineties, so doctors knew everything. We didn't have the social network we do now.

So I did. And we did.

I found out we were expecting around Thanksgiving. Instead of celebrating a joyous Christmas Eve by eating dinner with our family and opening gifts, we were in the ER having a miscarriage. Merry Christmas to us!

Once again, we were told that this happens to one in every five women and that we would probably never know why. We were also told to try again, right away.

I went back to work at my teaching position as soon as my doctor let me and threw myself into my work. A few weeks after my return, I suddenly became very dizzy and so tired that I could barely breathe. My principal sent me home with instructions to see my doctor. I went to my OB/GYN expecting to be told that I was anemic or something similar. Strangely, they could not find a thing wrong. I tried working but kept becoming dizzy and so fatigued that I became lethargic. These strange episodes kept happening with an increasing frequency that became scary.

I became more and more tired, until I was unable to function. I was unable to work, and I resigned from my teaching position.

I kept trying to do all the right things. I ate right. I got enough sleep. However, nothing helped, and the episodes kept happening. These episodes were horrible and only someone who is also suffering from them will fully understand how truly horrible they were. Mine began with feeling dizzy, then tunnel vision set in, next I would get the shakes, followed by nausea. I was terrified that I would either throw up in public or pass out. I saw either scenario as horrifyingly humiliating. These episodes began happening when I was out shopping or even buying stamps at the post office. Fear that I would have an episode while I was out gradually began to shrink my world smaller and smaller until one day, I realized that I hadn't been out of the house in a week. One week became four, then six, and before I knew it, I hadn't been out of the house alone in months.

During all this time, I kept going to my OB/GYN who kept finding nothing physically wrong. He finally referred me back to my GP. It didn't take her long to figure out that my nerves were shot and that I was emotionally exhausted. After discussing her findings with me, she shared them with my OB/GYN. He was an older doctor from a nearby small town and he simply did not find credence in her diagnosis. As a matter of fact, he told me that I was weak and needed to toughen up and go back to work like every other woman who had ever been in my shoes. It didn't occur to me that he didn't know every other woman who had ever been in my shoes. I was heartbroken and my self-confidence was crushed.

Luckily, my GP had other ideas. She referred me to a new OB/GYN who specialized in women who had experienced three or more losses of pregnancy. I emphatically told her that I did not want to try to get pregnant again for some time, therefore, I didn't need to go. She assured me that I most certainly did need to go because he would treat all of me, not just the baby making parts.

I reluctantly went and to my surprise and relief, he told me that the first thing he would do is make sure that I didn't get pregnant again until I was healthy, emotionally as well as physically. Next, he ordered tests to learn why I had the miscarriage. We knew why I lost the twins. He discovered that I had a rare condition that made my body fight the baby's heart as if it was a virus. The solution was that when I got pregnant again, I would need to take a baby aspirin daily. Simple enough.

He also told me that I needed to give my mind a break from worrying about being pregnant and losing another baby, and he diagnosed me as having panic and anxiety attacks. He told me to go home and allow myself to grieve. He told me to own the losses that we had experienced and to fully embrace it; all of it, the good times, the bad times, the horror, the sadness, and the fear. This part was not so simple.

He then told me to swing by our local library on our way home and check out everything they had on panic and anxiety attacks.

I did. I went by the library on the way home and checked out as much as they would let me, which at the time was seven books and 2 cassettes (yes, I am that old). Then I went home and stared at that pile of books for the next two weeks.

Facing what I was feeling was foreign to me. I had always either ran from how I felt or hidden it. Now I was just supposed to embrace it?

Little did I know then, as I stared at my stack of books, what an adventure this would be. I didn't know how much I would learn about myself. I didn't know where it would take me. I didn't know how it would be a therapy for my past and a hope for my future. I didn't know how it would strengthen my faith. I didn't know how it would take me from fearful to fearless.

If I had known then what I know now, I would have snatched up the first book and devoured it, right then, the very second that I got them in my hands and I would have not looked up until I had absorbed everything I would need to know to turn my life around, forsaking even food, drink and sleep for knowledge. Well, maybe I wouldn't have gone that far, but I would have dived right in.

When I did finally take that dive, I finally began feeling in control of the horrible episodes. I began feeling in control of myself and my life. I quickly learned that control is an illusion for the most part, but then so were the thoughts that caused my anxiety. **However, the one thing we can control is our reaction to the things we can't control.**

Fast forward a year or so and guess what? I am pregnant. You didn't skip a paragraph and you read that right. I was pregnant. I don't know how that happened, but for God, because I was taking the pill and getting birth control shots. (As I type this, the result of that pregnancy is asleep in his room, resting after a late night of studying for his college classes.)

I remember the moment I learned that I was pregnant as vividly as if it just happened. I had skipped a period and called my OB/GYN. He told me to take a pregnancy test, which I did. I knew that it would be negative and something else had to be going on. It was a good thing I didn't make a bet on what I "knew".

I remember calling him an hour later and telling him my surprising results in disbelief. What I remember the most is hearing his deep, belly laughs as he responded, "Well I guess God had other plans for you and for this baby."

Then I started crying. Did I want this baby? Yes! Emphatically, a million times over, YES! But I wasn't ready to be pregnant yet. Then my doctor quietly reassured me by saying, "I know you think you aren't ready for this, but you are. Now you have a choice. You can spend the next nine months crying and stressing out, not only yourself, but also this baby, over what you can't control, or you can take it one day at a time and use what you've learned and control how you feel about whatever happens." His words were so true, and daunting. He ended our conversation by reminding me that we now knew what had happened to result in not carrying to term in the past, and that we would do everything to prevent another loss. Bolstered by his words, I took a deep breath and decided to take it one day at time.

I quickly learned that one day at a time was too much. I adjusted my thinking, and instead took it one hour at a time. I could do an hour. An hour was easy. It was just sixty minutes. Once I handled that, I went to taking it three hours at a time and progressed from there. It wasn't long before I could go a whole day, then a week, and then even longer without stressing over the outcome.

I felt like a completely different person by the time I delivered my month son one month prematurely, yet still a chunk at nine and a half pounds, of little love. I didn't just feel like I was a different person because I was a mom. I felt like I was a different person because I tamed the beast that had been eating me alive.

Now that beast has shown up now and then but taming it has trained me in how to keep it tamed. Anxiety, much like alcoholism or being overweight, is managed more so than 100% completely cured. The good news is that once you have trained yourself to tame it, no one can take that away from you and you can use this skill in so many areas of your life to help make your life what you want it to be.

CHAPTER 2

MONSTER BASICS

◇◇◇◇

I don't want you to have to read this chapter in the same way that I don't want you to have to read dozens and dozens of books on anxiety, until you see the pattern of the themes in them as to what is causing your anxiety and how to stop it. It is time consuming. It can be very boring. It can be frustrating. It can even lead to more anxiety.

I want to condense the knowledge I have gained from the past three decades of learning and using anti-anxiety techniques and present it in an easy-to-read and, more importantly, easy-to-apply format.

Most of all, I want you feeling better now, not later. I want you to take control and feel in control of your life again. I want you excited about conquering this monster and ready to take on the world. I am in your corner and cheering for you!

To that end, I hope you took my suggestion to stop reading in Chapter 1, and went to the website I suggested, downloaded the recording, and have been listening to it. This will start you on the path to creating the life you want, a life undisrupted by anxiety.

Believe it or not, anxiety can be your ally as much as it can be your adversary. We will learn about making it our ally later on, but for now, we are going to do what we should all do when faced with what it is, an adversary. We are going to learn about it. Think of this as researching a frenemy on Facebook or stalking one on Instagram.

Chances are you already know the next information that I am sharing, and this chapter will just be a mini reference section for you.

Chances also are that you have already visited the internet looking for a solution to what you are experiencing or a remedy for your symptoms. If you have, you've learned that Dr. Google will tell you that anxiety can be a simple feeling of nervousness or develop into a profound mental disorder.

I disagree with the 'simple' part.

There is nothing simple about anxiety when you are feeling it. Dr. Google will also tell you that anxiety is caused by stress, leaving you to believe that stress is a bad thing, full stop, period.

What Dr. Google will not tell you is that there is a good form of stress, eustress. Eustress is defined as a moderate or normal psychological stress interpreted as being beneficial for the experience.

What experience could he (it) be referring to? Think of that feeling you get when you know you have a class or work project due. Perhaps you have decided to eat right and work out and you plan your meals and schedule your exercise. This feeling of anticipation or excitement is eustress.

Eustress helps you make changes. It helps you get things done. It comes from projects, assignments, or changes that are neither too easy nor too hard. It helps you prepare, perform and often, improve yourself. Eustress is **good** stress.

If you take away the 'eu' in eustress, you get stress. And stress without the 'eu' is bad. This stress happens when you feel an emotional or physical tension.

It is what happened to me in fourth grade when I worried about going through life without arms and being stared at. It is what happened again when I worried about my grandmother surviving without me for two weeks. And again when I worried about getting pregnant and having another loss. You get the picture.

You with me? Us mere mortals can have **stress, eustress, and distress**.

Distress, by definition, is extreme anxiety. Distress happens when we don't handle our stress. It quickly can take on a life of its own. This is what happened to me when I didn't deal with my loss in a healthy manner. My stress grew and grew, and my world became smaller and smaller.

We experience stress every day. It is a part of life. However, these are usually little stresses like someone cutting you off in traffic or forgetting to pick up milk at the grocery store. These are aggravating and frustrating, but they are little. They are an inconvenience and easy to handle and get over.

The stress that leads to anxiety happens when it becomes chronic. It is the stress that you don't handle properly or get over easily. For me, it was losing the twins and then having a miscarriage. I spent days, weeks, even months worrying about what if it were to happen again.

Anxiety took over my life and ruled it with an iron fist. I woke up dreading the moment when that horrible feeling of doom would start. I spent hours wondering how long it would last. I spent days exhausting myself with the 'what if' rollercoaster of up and down emotions. Anxiety controlled me.

It would take educating myself about anxiety and how it works to take my control back.

Now it is time for you to do the same.

If you have researched anxiety on Dr. Google, then this chapter will hopefully add to or continue your education. If this is your first venture into self-help for your problem, then welcome to class.

Let's review what we know and/ or need to know:

stress
/stress/

Noun - a state of mental or emotional strain or tension resulting from adverse or very demanding circumstances

eu·stress
/yoo'stres/

Noun - moderate or normal psychological stress interpreted as being beneficial for the Experiencer

dis·tress
/də'stres/

Noun - extreme anxiety, sorrow, or pain

But how does all this make you feel?

All we want is to feel good, right? However, these common anxiety signs and symptoms make us feel just the opposite.

Maybe you...

- feel nervous, restless, or tense
- or have a sense of impending danger or doom

ototototototотotototototototototototototototototototototototototototototototototototottotttttttttttttttttttttttttttttttttttttttttotttttttttttttttttttt

- have an increased heart rate
- are breathing rapidly (hyperventilation)
- are sweating
- are trembling
- feel weak
- feel tired
- have trouble concentrating
- have trouble sleeping
- have gastrointestinal (GI) problems
- can't control what you are worrying about.

…and left untreated, you will begin having the urge to avoid things that trigger anxiety!

Our goal is to stop all the above in its tracks so that it doesn't lead to…

ag·o·ra·pho·bi·a
/ˌagərəˈfōbēə/

Noun - extreme or irrational fear of entering open or crowded places, of leaving one's own home, or of being in places from which escape is difficult

Once you have agoraphobia, you have developed one of the Anxiety Disorders. Anxiety disorders are classified by the fear that created them. The 4 fears they are grouped under are:

- Catastrophic
- Evaluation
- Losing Control
- Uncertainty

If you have **Catastrophic** anxiety, you believe something bad will happen and constantly think thoughts pertaining to these bad things happening. Examples are Separation Anxiety and Specific Phobias. This is what I experienced when my family traveled, and I was separated from my beloved grandmother.

The most common type is **Evaluation** anxiety. In this, we fear being judged or evaluated. Social Anxiety stems from this type as does Selective Mutism, which occurs when we are scared to speak. I have seen numerous students exhibit this form of anxiety while I taught Pre-K.

Fears of **Losing Control** causes levels of anxiety that lead to panic disorders and can eventually lead to agoraphobia.

The fear of **Uncertainty** lives up to its name. It is the fear of the unknown. This fear can cause Generalized Anxiety Disorder and even OCD.

If you want to know more about these, feel free to refer to Dr. Google. The reason I am not going into them in more detail here is because while knowing the nitty gritty can help you stop anxiety, sometimes knowing more simply gives you more to worry about. We all have enough of that already.

Root Causes

No one plans on having anxiety. You didn't schedule a movie date with it. You didn't order it up at dinner one night so that you could taste it and see if you like it. Instead, you were going about your day and living your life when it showed up. The question is, why did it show up?

First, it didn't show up just for you. Sadly, you, and I, are not that special when it comes to anxiety. Anxiety is the most common mental illness. Anxiety also affects 30% of all humans.

The most basic explanation of anxiety is that our amygdala, which is the emotion center of the brain, is overly sensitive. I love this explanation because if it is overly sensitive, not only is our anxiety response stronger, but so is our love response, and our care response. I once had a therapist tell me that mean people rarely get anxiety. She went so far as to say that it is only the nicest people who have anxiety. You can see why I like this explanation.

There are many theories as to why anxiety happens. There is the Cognitive Theory, the Learning Theory, Nature versus Nurture theory, Trauma Theory, to just name a few. Again, if you want to know more about these, and there is nothing wrong with wanting to know the why of anything, please refer to Dr. Google. He can explain it much better and in implicitly more detail than I.

Whatever the cause, the effect is still the same. You have anxiety and don't want it. Now let's get rid of it.

CHAPTER 3

MONSTER TAMER IN TRAINING

⸻ ◇◇◇ ⸻

The bad news is that there are many reasons you can have anxiety. The good news is that there are only a few ways to treat it. Of course, there is medication. I had to forego the medication route because I was pregnant. Don't get me wrong. Initially, I resented my friends who could pop a pill and have that wonderful "help is on the way" feeling and breathe a "my level of anxiety is lowering" sigh. Then I watched them have episode after episode and require pill after pill and I knew that this was one of my life's biggest blessings. Being pregnant forced me to develop other anti-anxiety self-care that would be long-lasting and life-enhancing.

I didn't realize how truly blessed I was in this until I was counseling a friend. This was her take on anxiety medications. "I used meds for several years. I also dealt with the side effects of the meds for several years. The pros of medication are that it is a quick and easy fix. The cons are the side effects, and that you learn to rely on them, instead of developing strategies and techniques that allow you to be in control of yourself. I decided to jump off the medication wagon when I ran out of my med while my doctor was on vacation. I spent a miserable week without my handy dandy pill while waiting on him to return so that I could pop my peace, my calm, and my relaxation again. During that week, I was confident that he would return. However, the "what if" thought arose, "what if I couldn't get my pills anymore?". That thought grew into what if they stopped making them? What if the pill factory blew up? Etc. I knew these thoughts were not healthy and this showed me that it was time for a solution, not a band aid."

Her words showed me that while I didn't get to enjoy the quick "fix", I did. Instead, learn how to fix my own self anywhere, at any time, independent of anything else.

This brings us back to my visit with my new OB/GYN who just prescribed for me to swing by our local library on the way home and check out everything they had on panic and anxiety attacks.

To recap, I did. I went by the library on the way home and checked out as much as they would let me. I will tell you that taking that first step, opening that first book, helped me to begin feeling in control of the horrible episodes. This was a wonderful change from how I had been feeling.

I desperately needed a change.

I had been living a life of insecurity, fear, and unhealthy thoughts for two and half decades. This was the perfect Trifecta for a panic disorder.

To give myself a little bit of grace, I remind myself that this was the early 90's and people didn't talk about mental health back then. If you had a crazy Aunt Bessie, you kept her hidden away somewhere and she was talked about in hushed tones and whispers.

To add to the trifecta, both of my parents suffered from anxiety which meant I always had a 50% more chance of suffering from it than the average person. Next, you add the fact that I am a woman and women are twice as likely to get anxiety as men, and my chances of not having anxiety were smaller than the chance of having a snowball fight in Southeast Texas.

Before we get to how I got it gone, I want to let you know what was going on inside of me. It was horrible! It was scary! It made me miserable! And it all started with a thought!

- I thought a thought that made me feel nervous.
- That nervous feeling made my central nervous system think I was in danger.
- My adrenal glands flooded my body with adrenaline.
- My body began prepping itself to fight the danger or flee it.
- My heart began to race.
- My breathing sped up and began filling my lungs to capacity so they could fuel my thigh muscles.
- My muscles tensed, preparing to fight or flee.
- My pupils dilated to take in more of my surroundings.
- My peripheral vision would shrink so that I could focus better on the perceived threat.
- My mouth stopped salivating.
- My digestion stopped.
- My blood flow was diverting away from my skin to the muscles and organs that would need the extra oxygen to fight or flee.
- As the episode would begin to subside, fatigue and exhaustion caused by the exertion of the anxiety would set in.

This cascade of physical events would create feelings of panic. It made my body feel like it was full of pins and needles, caused stomach aches, headaches, tunnel vision, tinnitus, and made me sweat and feel chilled simultaneously.

This happened at the grocery store. It happened at the Post Office. It happened at work. And each time it happened, I began to overgeneralize that if it happened at each of these places, it could happen anywhere. My mind concluded that it was just safer to stay home. Home equaled safety. The only way I could leave my home was if my husband were with me.

In a noticeably short time, home came to feel as much of a prison as it did a safe haven, and my husband a jailer as much as he was the love of my life.

I did not want my child to grown up in a home that felt like a prison. I did not want him or her to see a mom who could not function in society, was not a productive member of society, and had to put undue stress and strain on his father, all because she was afraid of life.

Not wanting any of this, and wanting a rich full life, I stopped staring at my stack of books, and picked one up and opened it. Opening that book, opened my world.

I spent the next few months reading dozens of books. I learned something from each one. Sometimes it created an 'ah ha" moment, and sometimes it was just a nugget of information that added to my mental library of what it was going to take to be able to lead the life I wanted. *A life not spent staring at the same four walls.*

It only took a few books to see a pattern, a theme, as where I had gone wrong in my thinking process. Even though anxiety had many different symptoms, it started with one thing.

This thing is a thought. My thought, to be exact. I started the cascade of scary, horrible, miserable feelings by having a thought. A simple, complex, rational, and irrational thought. The thought could have been about anything. It could have been about nothing important. But the one thing it was doing was making me feel nervous. It took a long time to figure out how a thought could have brought all this on. I now call these thoughts 'what if" thoughts.

What if I lose my arms like the lady in the movie?

What if people stare at me using my feet for hands?

What if my grandmother needs me?

What if I need my grandmother and she is 3 states away?

What if I pass out?

What if my stomachache doesn't go away?

What if I feel worse?

What if I throw up in front of everyone?

What if this vomiting doesn't stop?

What if we get there and I want to leave and my ride doesn't?

What if I lose another baby?

What if? What if? What if? Forever, without end, amen!

These "what if" thoughts were continuously turning on my fight or flight response repeatedly. It would start the cascade of physical symptoms which made the "what if" thoughts change and increase.

What if I hyperventilate?

What if I lose control of myself in public and start screaming?

What if I pass out and someone robs or rapes me?

On and on the 'what if' merry-go-round went, and it wasn't so merry.

Then illumination dawned! I saw the light (and I don't mean THE light at the end of THE tunnel). I got it! For the first time, since all my problems with anxiety started, I completely and totally got it. If anxiety was started by a thought, then it could be stopped by a thought.

I had it! I got it!

Eureka! Boo-ya! Bazinga!

Then I lost it!

How do you stop it by a thought?

If my thoughts turn it on, how do I use my thoughts to turn it off?

CHAPTER 4

MONSTER TRAINER GOING PRO

—◇◇◇—

*A*ll that reading and studying that I had been doing worked great at bringing me general knowledge. Now I needed specific knowledge. How do I use my mind to work for me, instead of against me?

I began by tracking my anxiety. I noted the times and durations of my episodes. Then I rated them 1 to 10. 1 being that I could function and simply be aware that something was changing. Number 10 meant that I felt like I was about to totally lose control. I quickly noted that my anxiety **wouldn't** stay at a 10 for more than a minute or two at the most. As I dug deeper into my research on this, I learned that it **couldn't** stay that high for long. Our bodies are designed to fight or flee, and both are quick responses. Our adrenalin is made for the short track, not the marathon. Think of the cheetah. It can only run short distances because it, too, is made for a sprint, not a marathon. Another reason we can't maintain a 10 is because our emotions change too quickly. If I were to track the intensity of my episodes, they would look like a black and white line drawing of a roller coaster; up and down, then up and down again.

Praises be! *This* knowledge alone gave me hope. Once I knew that the intensity couldn't stay high, I knew that I could withstand it easier.

I soon noticed that as I told myself "so what" when my anxiety hit a 10, it would begin subsiding.

I quickly made the correlation that while "what if" turned it on, then "so what" was turning it off.

Next, I reached as far back into my memory as I could and journaled about all the previous episodes that I could remember. I gave each incident a name, then journaled its duration and intensity.

As I did this, I realized that I was missing a component. I had all the feelings down, but I had forgotten about the inciting factor; the thought that started it all. To correct this, I went back and added what I had been thinking before the anxiety started and what thoughts I had during the episode that made it continue.

The thought I had way back in fourth grade was easy. I had been sitting there thinking about what if I didn't have any arms, but in a negative context. Instead of thinking that I could be as industrious as the woman in the video, I was thinking about how I would feel so self-conscious at everyone staring.

Next, I analyzed what happened when I went on a trip and missed my grandmother. Instead of thinking about the fun I was about to have or having an indoor swimming pool at the hotel (yes, I am that country), I was focusing on the negative. I was thinking what if I have a stomachache while I am away from her or what if she needs me.

I began looking at my life and these anxious episodes a little bit differently. Then I began asking the hard questions.

My mind kept returning to the fact that there were twenty kids in that fourth-grade class and none of them seemed to have any issues while watching the documentary. My cousin had gone with us on that family trip as a playmate for me. She didn't have any problems being away from her grandmother. It took some more self-analyzation to figure it out.

I learned that my name was not the only unique thing about me. My brain, feelings, and emotions were too. Most of all, it was my childhood that set me up for my emotions to work so differently than others.

I was born with a double ear infection and suffered from such frequent and painful recurrences that I was one of the youngest babies at the time to get tubes inserted in my ears and adenoids taken out of my nose. I experienced these well into grade school and I can still remember the feeling of the infection coming on. Once the infection started, it meant a trip to the doctor for a shot to be followed by yucky medicine. This was so traumatic that I can remember the intense feelings of panic and dread that would come over me at the first hint that pain was coming.

The same thing happened when I felt the dizziness while watching that film. I certainly did not like the feeling and my nine-year-old brain quickly wondered how much worse it could get, which turned on the monster.

Next, I took a deep dive into the stomachache, nausea, vomiting cycle that I had experienced off and on for years. Sure enough, I could find a mental stressor that preceded each episode.

It was humiliating and empowering to know I had created this monster. It was humiliating to know that I was lacking the skills to properly navigate life like everyone else who didn't battle this Godzilla. But it was more empowering to know that I could truly stop it from destroying Japan, and me.

I had journaled the episodes that helped shape my life; a life I didn't want. I had analyzed them and critiqued them. I knew all that I needed to know about them and how they got me to where I was. Now what I needed to know was how to use that information to get me to where I wanted to be.

Fearless!

Peaceful!

Confident!

Courageous!

Productive!

Basically, everything that I currently felt I was not.

The desire to use the information that I had learned took me back to my newest discovery. The discovery of the power of "so what".

This was the answer. This was the big secret. This was the best answer and antidote. This was how I tamed the monster.

Yes, you read that right. Those two small words were how I tamed the monster that had me living in fear and afraid to leave my own home.

Don't take this nonchalantly. There is great power in these two words.

The words "what if" had wreaked havoc on my life.

The words "so what" would restore my life.

It was glorious knowing what I needed to do. Just like the words 'what if' and I formed a relationship; a negative one. Then the words 'so what' and I had to build one; a positive one.

This new relationship had to be just as strong and as intense as the old one was.

Just saying the words wouldn't do it.

I had to find a way to put some strength and passion into these words.

I had to train my monster to obey the new command that these words meant.

To do that, I had to train my mind. I had to teach it to see things in a positive light. I had to teach it that I wasn't going to be hurt every time I turned around. I had to teach it that the world was not a bad place. I had to teach it that it had done a good job up until now. It had done the best it could with what it knew. But now it was going to do a great job. Most of all, I had to teach it that it had done the best it could with what it knew, but it knew better now.

To go pro at training the monster, I began learning about what made the monster tick.

And just like that, we were back to the importance of thoughts.

I quickly learned that it did no good to say two positive words and have the rest of your words, especially those in your head be negative. The good news was that it took half as many positive words to balance out your negative ones as compared to the negative ones you thought or spoke to begin with.

The second thing I learned was that the human mind could not have two thoughts at the same time. We are a mono-thought being. Don't believe me? Try it.

We began the training in earnest the day I decided to drive around the block. I set a goal to be able to do this in 5 days. I started my training on a Monday and worked at it every day. The work wasn't hard, and it didn't take a long time.

By Friday, I was ready to perform what I had been training for. I got up and got dressed. Next, I picked up my purse and got my car keys out; keys that I hadn't used in 2 years. Then I walked down the sidewalk and climbed in my car. Finally, I started it, put it in gear, and drove around the block.

Tears filled my eyes as I completed my drive and pulled back into my parking spot. I put the car in park and sat there with my hands on the wheel. Those tears made their way down my cheeks. I felt like I had climbed Everest. I was so thrilled that I had done it, that I did it again; and again.

I finally parked the car and went inside after five or six trips. I was a little sweaty. I was a little shaky. But I had accomplished my goal. I was also grinning ear to ear. Go me! Woohoo!

I also had my next goal. For my next goal, I resolved to not only do this, but do it calmly and confidently.

I accomplished this goal even more quickly. I was driving around the block with ease in just three days. More importantly, I had just learned that the mind could not perceive the difference between reality and fantasy.

I began using my mind in the exact same way that I did when I watched TV or a movie. I watched something that made me feel like I wanted to feel. If I wanted to feel happy, I watched a comedy. If I wanted some drama, I watched a drama. If I wanted a thrill, I would watch a scary movie.

I imagined that I was doing whatever I had done before that I perceived to be frightening or scary, but this time I imagined it to be calm, or happy, or whatever I wanted to feel.

It worked and it worked every time. Not only could my mind not tell the difference, but my mind told my body that I had already done it and had experienced a positive outcome. This took away the worry. This took away the fear.

In less than two weeks, I was driving all over town. In less than a month, I flew across the country all by myself. I reclaimed my independence one outing at time.

Thus, my Monster Training Method was born.

CHAPTER 5

THE MONSTER TRAINING METHOD

◇◇◇

*T*his method not only got me out of the house and going, it also got me back in the classroom. I began teaching my students how to use this method to help them with everything from separation anxiety to test anxiety. I even taught my UIL Storytelling participants how to use this to eliminate stage fright and indecision when they competed. We rocked every event we entered and the looks on their faces as they walked away with first place ribbons was so rewarding. Eventually, I incorporated a five-minute morning meditation that set our class up for a wonderful day.

What you are about to learn has no limits. It doesn't go out of style or get old. I have been using it for over two decades and I just used it, in detail, to learn how to ride a motorcycle at 52. I took the Safety Class from our Cowboy Harley Davidson dealership in Beaumont, Texas. I passed. It was hard. It was nerve wracking. But I did it! It was scary because I had been on a motorcycle only once in my life. This was when a friend rode hers over to let me see it. I rode it that day and fell in love with the whole experience. I am so glad I did. Riding has brought me a new freedom and joy to my life.

Incorporate this in your life, and you can do anything. You can do hard things. You can do scary things. You can bring a whole new level of freedom and joy to your life just like I did.

An awesome fact about the brain is that it is like a muscle; the more you train it, the better it works. To train your muscles, you usually go somewhere special to do it. Maybe it is a gym, or maybe it is a workout room in your home. It can even be your living room if you have the right knowledge and the right workout equipment.

Our place to go to train our mind is our alpha state. This is not a physical place that we can walk or drive to. This is a mental state of consciousness.

Alpha is the level where your brain waves slow down to around half of the frequency they are while awake. We are going to use this state of mind because this is simply where the magic happens. It is where you train the monster.

Now don't get worried about finding this place or going there. You already do this several times a night, or day if you work nights. Have you ever been in that place between awake and sleep and it feels wonderful? The weight of the world hasn't descended upon your mind yet, and the warm comfort of sleep still has you wrapped in its soothing embrace. This is the alpha state. In this state, we often have amazing ideas or find the solution to a problem we are having that comes to you suddenly, out of nowhere. It is coming to us from the alpha state. We go through this state on our way to deep sleep, which is the delta state, and when we come awake, this is our beta state.

In alpha, your blood pressure normalizes, your heart rate stabilizes, and your stressed organs recuperate from the wear and tear they have taken from your day. Most importantly, you have reached an inner conscious level where you can tell your body and mind what you want it to feel and how you want it to think.

Learning this has been so much more than an "ah-ha" moment for me. This was an eureka, mind blowing, Katie-bar-the-door, earth shattering moment.

The best news of all is that not only can we train ourselves to easily get to our alpha state with a few techniques, but we can also get better at it with practice. It will also become easier and easier, the more we do it.

I began by doing this after waking up, around noon, and then at bedtime. I was enjoying the full effects of agoraphobia at the time (said no one ever), therefore all I had was time and I put that time to good use.

First, decide how you want to feel and what thoughts you want to think in any situation. This will usually be the opposite of the feelings that led you to read this book. I would picture myself driving and thinking calm and self-confident thoughts and feeling calm and self-confident.

Then,

1. Sit or lay in a comfortable position.
2. Focus on your feet and take a slow and controlled deep breath in that fills your belly. Tighten all the muscles in your feet, and then simultaneously let the breath out and relax your feet.
3. Focus on your lower legs from right above your knees on down and take a slow and controlled deep breath in that fills your belly. Tighten all the muscles in this area, and then simultaneously let the breath out and relax your lower legs.
4. Focus on your thigh muscles and take a slow and controlled deep breath in that fills your belly.

Tighten all the muscles in your thighs, and then simultaneously let the breath out and relax your thigh muscles.

5. Focus on the area from your belly button down to the top of your thighs and take a slow and controlled deep breath in that fills your belly. Tighten all the muscles in this area, and then simultaneously let the breath out and relax this area.

6. Focus on your back from the base of your neck to the top of your hips and take a slow and controlled deep breath in that fills your belly. Tighten all the muscles in your back, and then simultaneously let the breath out and relax your back.

7. Focus on your front from the top of your shoulders to the bottom of your belly and take a slow and controlled deep breath in that fills your belly. Tighten all the muscles in your front. Feel the tightness in your chest muscles and in your stomach muscles. Then simultaneously let the breath out and relax all this area.

8. Focus on your neck paying special attention to the back of your neck. We tend to hold much of our stress and anxiety here and take a slow and controlled deep breath in that fills your belly. Tighten all the muscles in your neck, and then simultaneously let the breath out and relax your neck. Roll your head from side to side and enjoy how relaxed your neck feels.

9. Focus on the back of your head, all the way up and over the top of your head to your hairline. Take a slow and controlled deep breath in that

fills your belly. Tighten all the muscles in this area, and then simultaneously let the breath out and relax your head.

10. Focus on your face, paying special attention to your forehead and jaw. Take a slow and controlled deep breath in that fills your belly. Tighten all the muscles in your face, and then simultaneously let the breath out and relax your face.

11. Focus on your eyes and the tiny muscles surrounding your eyes. Take a slow and controlled deep breath in that fills your belly. Squeeze your eyes shut as tight as you can and tighten the muscles surrounding your eyes. Then simultaneously let the breath out and relax this area.

Now you are in the alpha state or close enough to it.

Next, focus on how you want to feel and what thoughts you want to think in as you handle any situation or are going about your day. The key here is detail. You have probably heard the old adage that the devil is in the details. For our purposes, the control is in the details. The more detail that you use when imagining how you want to feel, the more your mind thinks you have already done it and therefore knows how to do it a second time.

Visualize yourself in the situation. Fully immerse yourself in the moment. Picture the look on your face as you gain control of your nerves.

After you have done this, tell yourself mentally that when you count to five, you will feel wide awake and wonderful.

Stay in this state for as long as you feel productive in it, then count to five and open your eyes and stretch, or yawn, or do whatever feels natural to you.

Congratulations! You have just programmed you mind. You have taken the first step in training the monster to mind you instead of your body minding it.

The end all, be all answer to anxiety is to exchange your 'what if' thoughts to 'so what' thoughts!

This seems too good to be true, doesn't it?

This feels too simple to work, right?

However, **IT DOES**! And it will always work for you. The more you do it, the better the results and the better you will get at it.

Now don't get me wrong. You can make this as hard or complex as you want it to be. The choice is yours, and yours alone.

As I used it, I first got out and about driving by myself. Next, I went shopping and running errands by myself. Then I flew across the country by myself. After that, I used this technique for maintenance, to keep myself from falling back into old habits.

Now don't be surprised if a "what if" thought rears its ugly head. You simply tame it by using your "so what" thought.

Note: There are additional Monster Training Scripts in Chapter 12.

CHAPTER 6

MONSTER ANTICS

◇◇◇

"To be in control of your body,
you must first be in control of your mind."
Jose Silva

*J*ust like any dog will try to get the treat without performing the behavior that earns it the treat, thus reverting back to prior training behavior, your monster will do the same. And just like it takes a firm command to get your pooch to perform correctly again, it can take using a firm command with your monster for it to do the same.

After beginning my monster training, I wanted to go to a friend's kickboxing match. First, I went through all the questions. Do I really want to go? What happens if I get there and start feeling bad? Will my husband be angry if I want to come home? Yadda, yadda, yadda. You probably know all too well what I mean.

This was the first time the rubber met the road, so to speak, for me. I had to slow my roll and ask myself; how do I want to feel about even making this decision? The answer was that I wanted to feel confident. I wasn't deciding to go to the moon, for Pete's sake. I was simply deciding whether or not to go watch a friend annihilate someone in the ring. I took a deep breath and visualized this and did it. I decided to go.

At the last minute, we decided to go with friends. Look out world! This brought up a new problem! Now it wouldn't just inconvenience my husband if I started panicking, it would also inconvenience our friends. And horror of horrors, they might actually see me having a panic attack. Again, I had to go back to my relaxation and visualization. Guess what? I STILL WANTED TO GO!

So, we went. I could feel that old familiar feeling begin as we drove there. My brain went to "what if…what if… what if."

To retaliate, I would firmly, and in my "don't mess with me," inner voice say, "so what!" In the beginning of this outing I had to do this every fifteen-minutes. But as the day went on, I didn't need it so often. By the time my friend entered the ring, I didn't need to do it at all.

Did this take a mental toll? You bet! But it wasn't anything I couldn't handle. The minor fatigue I felt from battling my own emotions was nothing compared to the joy I felt at taming my monster. I was exhilarated.

Later that evening, as I journaled my day, I made the connection that when I was afraid of what I was feeling, the feeling increased, and when I wasn't afraid of it, it decreased and eventually went away.

Was this the magic pill that once taken would last me the rest of my life? Heck no!

"The best intentions are fraught
with disappointment."
Gil Grissom, CSI Las Vegas

"The only constant God ever
created was change."
Rebell Wade

Life changes in an instant and we will always encounter things that are going to make us feel nervous and anxious. However, this is a tool that we can use each and every day to help us enjoy our life and live it to the fullest.

I have used this for taming small monsters like…

- Driving in bad storms
- Driving in Houston traffic
- Dental appointments
- MRI's
- Work meetings

I have used this for taming big monsters such as…

- Job interviews
- Proficiency tests
- Court depositions
- Root canals
- Back surgery
- ***HEALING MY BODY***

That last bullet point is in all caps, bold, italics, and a larger font because I thought using Monster Training was just to help me get over anxiety and agoraphobia, little did I know that it would have a much larger purpose in the years to come.

While I learned this in my mid-twenties, it wasn't until I was forty that it saved more than my mental state. It saved my life.

I had either caught mono or had a flare when I was forty. We do not know which. Some of my doctors think that I had it as a young child or teen and that it simply wasn't diagnosed correctly since I was such a sickly child. Others thought this was my first bout of it. Either way, it almost ended my life. I went from relatively healthy and living life large, to sleeping twenty hours of my day away. It took several weeks to get a diagnosis of mono, either flare or new condition, and steroids were started. Steroids that didn't help me at the time, and later caused a bigger problem

By the time I began recovering, which only happened when I took matters into my own hands and is documented in my book The Best Mono Cure, the virus had ruined my adrenal glands. I now had adrenal fatigue. Adrenal glands are some of the smallest glands in the human body, yet they run most of the body. When they are not working correctly you feel worse than miserable. You actually feel like you are dying. You heart and respiratory system do not work together, and you feel like you are swimming backwards, and upside down, while trying to breathe through mud. You hurt all over and feel lethargic.

I was told it would take months to recover from this. I was determined to do it in weeks instead. I began researching holistic approaches to help me recover and began implementing them into my life.

I also tweaked my Monster Training script to incorporate sayings that would help my body heal. Now I focused on feeling healthy and well. I would get incredibly detailed and picture myself waking up energetic and strong. I would picture myself having energy and moving around free of pain.

After several days, my health began turning around and my doctors were amazed at how quickly I recovered.

I had a few good months, then I started experiencing a strange fatigue that went far beyond the usual tiredness of 'teacher tired'. Most people don't realize that teaching, especially elementary school teaching, is very tiring. You are not only teaching, you are mothering, nursing, coaching, feeding, counseling, refereeing, and even sometimes ministering to kiddos, while always supervising them. Did I mention ALWAYS supervising them? No wonder teachers are tired and have a high burnout rate.

I went in for more testing. The results showed that my adrenals had not recovered. The adrenal fatigue had progressed into Congenital Adrenal Hyperplasia.

I was told that my life would be a big circle of fatigue and lethargy for the rest of my life.

I was told that I could go acute and die in my sleep at any time.

I was told that I would be steroid dependent for the rest of my life.

I was told I would have continuous weight gain for the rest of my life.

Have any of these things happened?

Nope! Nadda!

Have I had to work at them not happening?

You betcha! That work consists of doing my own research, finding and using whatever works from holistic remedies to pharmaceutical ones, being my own advocate, but mostly using my Monster Training technique. Remember that I said that life happens and our stressors change? This was a huge stressor and I have managed it for over a decade.

I have energy and feel normal most of the time. (But no one feels normal all the time!)

I haven't died (obviously).

I've been able to get off steroids after being dependent on them for 10 years. (I am 2 ½ years steroid free.)

I may not be at the weight I want, but I also don't weigh the four hundred pounds my doctors predicted.

I've taught Pre-K and Fourth Grade!

I ride a motorcycle.

I live my life to the fullest.

I share what I have learned.

Beating the odds has been made possible by Monster Training. Ditto, living a full life.

I have had to adopt the philosophy of progress not perfection, and everyday isn't sunshine and roses. But every day is doable, and not only do I find a reason to smile, but I learn something. If you aren't learning, you aren't' living.

I've trained the monster on good days.

I've trained the monster twice as hard on bad days.

I've forgotten or neglected to train the monster for several days, here and there, and had to deal with the consequences.

However, I have never taken training the monster for granted. I am so thankful that my life experiences led me to learn this because it has enhanced my daily life.

I was never so glad that practice makes perfect, or almost perfect, as I was when I had to have emergency back surgery. One year I was teaching Pre-K when a four-year-old severely damaged my back. This four-year-old was quite large and ran into our classroom one morning very excitedly. I was squatting down on my heels, tying another child's shoes when he leapt at me to give me a hug. He knocked me down on my rear end, but more weight landed on my left side. My bum didn't have more than eight inches to fall, but it fell with seventy-five pounds of kiddo on top of me. (Yes, you read that weight right.)

My little friend got his hug and we laughed about my tumble as I got to my feet. It wasn't until after work that I realized something was wrong. My husband and I were working out at our gym. I was walking on the treadmill and he was in the weights section. Suddenly my lower body locked up and pain began shooting down the back of my right leg. Instead of my normal stride, I could now barely shuffle my feet. I sent someone to fetch him and we went to the emergency room. The doctor at the emergency room immediately gave me an anti-inflammatory shot, a script for muscle relaxers, and sent me to have an MRI. The MRI showed that L4 and L5 had been severely damaged. Luckily, a spine specialist from Houston had an office in Beaumont on Thursdays and was willing to fit me in and see me. We went straight over and he performed a nerve conduction test. Just in case you've never heard of this, it is when they stick thin needles into your muscles to see how well your nerves are relaying information through the body. My body would respond on my left side normally. The right side was a different story. Not only did they insert the needles at maximum depth, but they also used maximum electricity. On the left side, I could feel the needles at the depth of half an inch and with their machine setting of two. I had no feeling on the right.

The doctor came into the room after the test and gave us the result of the MRI and the nerve conduction test. The bad news was that I needed emergency surgery. The even worse news was that since the emergency room doctor had just given me an anti-inflammatory injection, I really shouldn't have surgery for a week. The worst news of all was that I didn't have a week.

All the test results showed that L4 and L5 had sheared off the "horse tail" nerves that work your legs. These literally look like a horse's mane where they go through the spine. If I didn't have surgery, I could be paralyzed. I needed surgery to put the discs back in place immediately. Surgery would stop the pain, but the doctor told me that I only had a fifty percent chance of regaining feeling in my right hip and leg, at best.

After consulting with his medical team, it was decided that it would be too risky to perform surgery that night or even in the morning. Since it was a Thursday night, he sent me home with explicit instructions to go home and sit. He told me to get up only to use the bathroom. I was to eat and sleep in my chair. He looked me up and down and told me to not even shower and that he expected to see me in the same clothes I had on when he met me at his office in Houston at five in the morning the following Monday. I must have made a face at this last instruction because he sternly told me that he was not joking, and gave me a red plastic card that had his personal number on it and instructions for what to do if I lost control of my bowels or bladder. I was to call him and he would have me life flighted to his hospital. Evidently, losing control of either of those things were the precursor to being paralyzed. He had my full attention now.

We left and I was in a state of shock and terror. Back surgery is a big deal! Huge! My anxiety went through the roof as we went home. I had a good crying fit, then my monster training kicked in with a vengeance. This was Thursday and Monday was three days away. I did not want to spend those days having panic attack after panic attack. I couldn't change the fact that I needed emergency surgery, but I could certainly control how I reacted to that knowledge. I got home and followed his instructions immediately. I sat in my chair and the first thing I did was my relaxation, and I began telling my mind how I wanted to think and feel. Not only did the Monster

Training stop the anxiety, it also helped with the pain. On a scale of 1 to 10, my pain had been at a 10+++, afterwards it would only go as high as a 4 or 5.

I made it through the weekend and looked forward to having the surgery over and done with. We got up at three in the morning on Monday and drove to Houston. My doctor met me at the door with a smile a mile wide and a "happy" shot in his hand. He told me that he truly didn't expect me to make it through the weekend but was so glad that I did. Within moments they had me feeling pain free and happy.

The surgery went perfectly, and we went home that same day. Once home, the only pain relief I needed was a couple of acetaminophens for a sore incision. It was wonderful to not only go through this calm and relaxed, but to also come out of this not needing any prescription pain meds.

Once home, I used my Monster Training to help my body heal. I was allowed a month off of work to recuperate, I only needed two weeks. Let's face it, four-year old's need their teacher, not a substitute. My spine doctor was amazed when I went to my six weeks checkup. He said that my recovery looked more like a six-month recovery than just six weeks. He asked how I had managed it and when I told him, he replied, "If more people used this, my job would be tremendously easier."

My spinal surgery goal was to be able to squat down to tie tiny shoes for tiny kiddos again. I was able to do that, without pain, two months post-surgery.

Feeling my right hip and leg took a bit longer. It took a year and half, but the feeling did come back, and that was all that mattered.

CHAPTER 7

MONSTER TRAINING THE MASSES

◇◇◇

> "You will never change your life until
> you change something you do daily.
> The secret of your success is found
> in your daily routine."
> John C. Maxwell

Professional athletes know that you don't win the game on the field or court. You win in practice, before the game ever starts. Athletes also know that you need to practice like you are playing and play like you practiced.

Life is the ultimate game. Those who practice, do better than those who just take the field or court and hope for the best.

After I learned how to practice what I wanted to think and how I wanted to feel, I learned that to win in the game against anxiety, I needed to help others.

Unfortunately, I had to start with my own family. There is a lot of controversy over whether anxiety is genetic or learned. Knowing this, we made sure that our first born never saw me have an anxiety attack. Needless to say, it took us by surprise when he began showing signs of anxiety at a young age. We promptly took him to a psychologist who informed us that most medical professionals believe that anxiety can be equally genetic or learned or a combination of both. My point is that we did everything in our power to make sure our son's anxiety was not learned.

However, at the age of four, he was diagnosed with Generalized Anxiety Disorder(GAD). And just like we followed his pediatrician's recommendations to treat his chronic bouts of strep and ear infections, we followed his psychologist's treatment for GAD. We learned that he would need new skills and strategies to deal with anxiety every time that he entered a new phase of growth. Sure enough, just like clockwork, when it was time for new jeans, due to a growth spurt, it would also be time for new techniques to keep him mentally healthy and happy. We joke about his phases now, but the point is, he *can* joke about it.

When he was around ten, he came to me one morning after seeing a Gardasil commercial, and told me he wanted the vaccine because he didn't want to catch cervical cancer. This was after the vaccine had just been approved and long before they gave it to boys as well as girls. I explained why he didn't need it and he laughed feeling relieved.

Next, he went through a phase where he could not see a dead body on television. This was hard for our NCIS, CSI and Criminal Minds loving family. However, it wasn't long after he grew out of this that he decided he wanted to become an FBI agent because "DB's don't bother me anymore."

I could tell you a dozen more stories just like this one, but I would rather tell you that this little kid who was diagnosed with GAD at four, is now wrapping up grad school after earning a double major in Psychology and Criminal Justice. After he has his master's degree in Criminal Justice, he plans on going to law school.

Our son has flourished and is a mentally healthy young man all because we gave him the skills he needed to manage his anxiety and his life.

Luckily, our daughter did not have the same problems as our son, but anxiety touched her life also. We were at a select softball practice in a nearby town when she was fourteen. I was sitting in the stands with the other sports moms when I happened to look over at the dugout. She had the strangest look on her face. I got up, walked over, and motioned for her to come to the fence. I could tell her breathing was irregular as she walked over. I quietly asked her what was going on and she informed me that she felt strange and wanted to leave. I told her to get her stuff and meet me at the car while I let her coach know what was going on.

When she climbed in, I looked into her fear-filled eyes and dramatically said, "Welcome to the family, Oh Anxious One." She looked at me first in horror, then in understanding. Next, she burst into a combination of tears and laughter. We went to get a bite to eat and I explained the ins and outs of Monster Training. She began using relaxation techniques and didn't have another issue until she was sixteen.

Now this one is hilarious, after the fact, of course, and it became legendary in our huge select softball community. My daughter was playing in a tournament one weekend in Houston. It started on a Friday, so her coach picked her up from the school where I worked as a teacher and took her with him and his daughter. She was going to stay with them until I could meet them the following morning. Then it started to rain. We had storms and downpours and our area became flooded. My daughter became concerned that I wouldn't be able to make it to her the next morning. Added to this worry, they played horrible during their evening game. Coach yelled. My daughter started feeling tense because she thinks everyone should be on top of their game and some of her teammates weren't. The game ended and they were walking back to Coach's truck when she called me. I could hear the panic in her voice right away. I told her to hand her phone to Coach. When he got on, I explained to him that she was having a panic attack and to follow my instructions. I told him to hold up two fingers in front of her face and move them up and down, then side to side, with no discernable pattern. Coach is listening to me and following my directions while asking my daughter if she is okay, every few minutes. Coach was beginning to get a bit more anxious than my daughter and I asked him how he was doing. He answered with a terse, 'Fine. I'm just fine." Finally, I heard her start laughing.

I knew she was going to be fine as soon as she started laughing. I explained to Coach why I had him do what he did and how it helped her. He then gave her back her phone and I spoke to her for a few minutes. As we were wrapping up, I heard the assistant coach speaking in the background. He asked Coach what was going on. I could hear Coach explaining. Then I heard the assistant coach comment, "Thank God! I walked up and saw you making the sign of the cross in front of her and I thought she done went possessed!" Yes, he said it just like that. And we all howled with laughter.

Now on to a more serious story. Fast forward to January 10, 2020. My husband of twenty-eight years had a heart attack. They performed an angioplasty and told us he needed open heart surgery. The morning after telling us this, they did two more tests and amended their treatment to him just needing a stent inserted. The next day, they did another angioplasty and put the stent in. Shortly after placing the stent, he coded. His blood pressure had bottomed out and they had to add more fluids to raise it. It took forty-five minutes before he was able to stay responsive. After he came to, the doctors explained to him what had happened. At bedtime that evening, the stress of everything caught up to him and he had his first panic attack ever. His heart/vitals monitor showed that he was getting agitated. This brought his nurse in. She checked him out and said she was going to call the doctor so that he could order him something to help him relax. I asked her to wait for a bit. I then talked him through a relaxation and Monster Training session. She came in forty-five minutes later to find him sleeping peacefully. She asked me what changed, and I explained to her what we did. She asked me to repeat the process several times so that she could remember it for future use then stated that she wished all of her patients knew how to do it.

The uses for Monster Training are limitless.

One of my favorite uses for Monster Training is for depression. I have taught my friends who suffer from depression how to use it to improve and heal. The feedback I have gotten from them has been phenomenal. Each one of them has reported that it has helped them in some way. Most have reported marked improvement after just a few days.

My daughter has used it to not only improve her softball game, but also to win the base she wants to play. She would try out for select team after select team, working her way up from the lower status teams to the top ones. My daughter wants to play first base. She is a lefty with an amazing stretch and owns this base like a boss. However, all the teams already have a first baseman so she would have to battle for it. This means that she would have to play the base for an extended period of time and make less errors than the current first baseman.

Battling for a base can take time. You have to prove why you should have the base instead of the other player. She would use Monster Training to visualize herself winning the base and playing it error free. She would visualize the coach watching her with satisfaction. She would envision great balls coming her way that showcased her abilities. Most of all, she would envision herself winning the base quickly. It never took her longer than three weeks to earn first base no matter how long the current first baseman had been playing it. This is a perfect example of how powerful the mind is and how easily you can train your mind like my daughter trained her body to throw and catch softballs.

My son has used it to ace tests.

My students have used it improve their learning experiences and ease their test anxiety.

My students with behavior issues have used it to help them improve their behaviors.

My Storytelling students have used it to win first place in UIL competitions.

I have used it to heal my mind.

I have used it to heal my body.

I have used it to create the life I want to live.

You can use it for all of the above, as well as job interviews, medical tests, dental appointments, surgeries, etc. You can use for any situation that you find yourself in where you may feel nervous or anxious.

CHAPTER 8

THE HIGH COST OF KEEPING YOUR MONSTER

◇◇◇

What you are not changing, you are choosing!

As you begin taking control of your anxiety, you will come across many other people that also have anxiety, yet have no desire to help themselves, ease their anxiety, or to put it simply, get better.

This has always boggled my mind. Having anxiety is hard. Recovering from anxiety is hard. One leads you to a full life of unlimited potential. One leaves you with an unfulfilled and limited life. So why do some people choose the latter? Sadly, many will find it easier to stay where they are than work to where they want to be. They will live a life wondering how good life could be. They will wonder what they are missing. Most of all, they will wonder what they are losing by living their life the way they do. Some will lose money, others will lose family, friends, or relationships. Some will lose their freedom...or their lives from addictions.

Another reason that people choose to stay stuck where they are is that they get something out of it. Let's face it, we do get something out of having anxiety. We get attention. We get an easy out. If we don't want to do something, all we have to say is, "Gee, I am having some anxiety, so I really don't want to go fill in the blank, or do fill in the blank."

The question is, "Is it worth it be stuck with how yucky you feel, to be able to get attention or take the easy way out, which is already yours if you just own it?" It was a whopping big NO! for me, and I've never looked back.

Not only can not taming your monster limit your life, it can and will affect your health if left untreated. There are several health dangers that are aggravated by stress. These include but are not limited to:

- Adrenal disease – More about this one below
- Cardiovascular disease – chronic stress has long been associated with heart attacks by adding wear and tear on the heart as it races and calms
- Hypertension – both acute and chronic stress have been linked to high blood pressure
- Diabetes - both acute and chronic stress have been linked to a rise in blood sugar levels
- Depression
- Cancer
- Insomnia
- Colds and infections - both acute and chronic stress have been linked to lowered immunity
- Asthma
- Obesity
- Gastrointestinal problems

The simple truth is that stress can aggravate any physical condition you have. The body is made to self- heal, given the right circumstances. The first step for this to happen is to reduce or remove stress. Mindset matters! Most physicians believe that the body can recover from most ailments with the right mindset, enough rest, and quality nutrition, without any medical intervention. Training your Monster is a win-win!

Allow me to keep it real for moment, really personal. I have often wondered what part all the stress and anxiety I endured as a child, teenager, and young adult, added to the damage done to my adrenals. I also wonder how different my life would be if I had learned to tame the monster at an earlier age.

CHAPTER 9

TAKING THE MONSTER TO CHURCH

⟡⟡⟡

L et's talk about religion. I know it is taboo. I simply don't care. Religion has done its fair share of damage to not only mental health, but also to the mental health field.

Religion tells us that your faith should be stronger than your fear. It doesn't take into account the science our bodies are going though.

Religion tells us that God can and will cure us but doesn't tell us that sometimes God's way of helping us is leading us to ways to help ourselves.

Religion tells us that if we have any mental illness, we are weak. It doesn't promote us being proactive to make ourselves strong.

Religion tells us that if we have anxiety, we aren't going to church, or fasting, or praying, enough.

Religion tells us that we shouldn't need or go to psychologists or psychiatrists.

Religion can make you feel ashamed of how you feel, yet if you believe in God and that God created everything, then you have to believe that God created the very feelings that religion wants you to be ashamed of. This one alone never made sense to me.

While learning to train my monster, I realized that I had to train myself out of some not so helpful religious training. I had to train myself out of believing that God was just watching and waiting for me to be bad or mess up. I had to train myself out of believing that God had the hellfire and brimstone in hand, just waiting to be hurled at me in the form of bad experiences.

I am sure you have heard at least one self-righteous person say, maybe even to you, that if your faith were strong enough, you wouldn't have anxiety. I have had to train myself to have a little self-righteousness of my own and respond by quoting Matthew 5:45. They have no response when you ask, "Then why does the Bible say it rains on the just and the unjust alike?"

What good is religion then? I can think of only one thing religion is good for, and that it is that it leads you to spirituality.

After I got off the religious path, I had to decide what I did believe in. This let me to my spiritual path. This is one of the best things that has come out of having anxiety. What a wonderful journey this started me on that I am still enjoying to this day.

While journaling my anxious thoughts, I realized that one of my biggest stressors was my fear of dying. I then analyzed why this was. Next, I began studying death and dying. Not only was this an interesting topic, but it also helped me decide what I believe happens when we physically die. This belief deepened into the faith I now have about what happens when we leave this physical world for the spiritual one, and my fears associated with death and dying are gone.

I am often asked how I got from feeling terrified at the thought of dying to being completely comfortable with it now. The answer is simple. I used my Monster Training techniques.

Whenever I had a spiritual question, I would do my Monster Training relaxation and visualize myself feeling the question deep in my soul. Then I would visualize the answer coming to me in a way that knew that it was from God and only God. This taught me how really true the old adage, "when the student is ready, the teacher will appear," is. It worked each and every time and my spirituality grew with each question that I asked.

CHAPTER 10

MONSTER BITS & PIECES

◇◇◇◇

(These are little nuggets of information
that I have learned along the way
that help me manage my life.)

On Going Home

Home is not a place; it is a feeling. I spent entirely too much of my younger life waiting to either go home or be home. Home was my safe place. Home was where the anxieties of the world didn't weigh too much on me.

Ironically, I experienced anxiety while at home also. The difference was that people couldn't see me and it alleviated some of the fear I had of losing control in public.

However, it isn't feasible to stay home all the time. It isn't emotionally healthy to not have some variety. It isn't physically healthy to not be exposed to germs so that you can build up your immunity. It isn't spiritually healthy not to communicate and fellowship with our fellow humans, no matter how much they get on our nerves.

The trick is to carry a piece of home with you wherever you go. This can be a state of mind, or something tangible. It can be a piece of jewelry, an article of clothing, or even a small towel or blanket. Whatever item you choose should bring you comfort when you think about it, see, or touch it.

I took my beloved grandmother's old, long-sleeved, denim shirt with me. If it was hot, I would just throw it over my arm. If it was cool enough to wear, I would use it in place of a jacket. My grandmother wore it while working in the yard on cool days. I can still picture her with a rake in her hands, wearing this shirt. I have had it for over twenty years, and I am even wearing it now while I am writing this, on this cool October morning.

Creating Safe Relationships

Choose to be with people who are good for your mental health. This applies to family members also. You can't control how other people act, but you can control your reaction to them. Don't give your mental health away to anyone. If they don't have your best interest at heart, then they don't need to have access to you. Boundaries are a wonderful thing.

Take Out the Trash

Everyone's body is different, but I learned early on that what I put into mine had a huge impact on how I felt. If I had too much sugar or caffeine, it would make me jittery and start the 'what if' thoughts.

I even had to watch what I put in my mind. If I watched an emotionally upsetting show or movie, my breathing would change, and that old anxious feeling would start.

Alcohol is a depressant that depresses your central nervous system for a while, but when it wears off, this false calm tends to reverse with a vengeance and while drinking an alcoholic beverage may not affect me when I drink it, the after effects can bother me for up to twenty-four hours.

Anxiety Products

The good news about living in an anxiety riddled world is that there are many products available to help sufferers. These products include:

- Fidget Spinners
- Essential Oils designed for anxiety (2 of my favorites are Peace & Calm from Young Living and Lavender EO from Plant Therapy)
- Weighted Blankets (Sam's Club sells a blanket that is not marketed as a weighted blanket but weighs around 6 pounds. It is sold at Christmas time for around $30. It is the perfect weight to start out with and one side is fleece and one furred, both soothing to the senses.)
- Relaxation and Meditation recordings that you can listen to on YouTube for free or that can be downloaded from private sites for a reasonable price
- Binaural Beat therapeutic recordings
- Blue and white light glasses

You don't have to limit yourself to one product or technique. I am a big believer in using what works for you and using as many as you need.

Ground Yourself

Grounding is an incredibly old technique to center and calm yourself. It can be done anywhere and done mentally.

1. Sit or stand comfortably.
2. Take 3 slow breaths with your eyes closed.
3. Open your eyes and notice 3 things you can see.
4. Notice 3 things you can touch.
5. Notice 3 things you can smell
6. Notice 3 things you can taste.
7. Notice 3 things you can hear.
8. Notice how calm and relaxed you feel now.

Own Your State

One of my biggest downfalls while learning techniques was to not own how I was feeling. I kept my feelings a better secret than who shot Kennedy. It was as if admitting my feelings would either make me feel them stronger or make me appear weak by admitting I felt anything less than normal Now I know that normal is just a setting on the washing machine. Ironically, I learned that sharing that I was feeling anxious with someone immediately started decreasing the level of it. Also, many would tell me about times when they felt anxious and how they helped themselves. Not only did I learn new techniques, but it felt glorious to not feel so alone in what I was going through.

Affirm Yourself

One of my favorite ways to combat stress and anxiety is to put affirmations up in different areas of my home, at work, and in my car. I use dry erase markers and write anything from Bible verses to uplifting quotes or memes on my bathroom mirror and even on the back of my front door. I like to have something positive to think about as I go out into the world.

Some of my favorites are:

What you allow to continue, will!

Worrying is like running on a treadmill! Just wears you out but takes you nowhere.

You can't control the world, but you can control your reaction to it.

Grateful! Thankful! Blessed!
Find calm in the chaos.
Happy is a choice.
Isaiah 40:31
Isaiah 41:10
Psalm 94:19
Psalm 34:4
Isaiah 34:4
Psalm 56:3
1 Peter 5:7
Psalm 23rd
My personal favorite is Isaiah 54:17.

Tell Me Something Good

When I began researching what to do to feel better, one of the first things I realized was that the news made me more anxious. I stopped watching the news and instead would read a story from the Chicken Soup for the Soul books. Replacing negatives with positives made a huge difference in how my day went.

Taking this a step further, as a teacher, I would find the right moment in the middle of class to bust out my moves and sing the Chaka Khan refrain, "Tell me something good," and point to a student. That student had a few seconds to share something good that had happened to them. Then I would sing it again and point to another student. I would repeat this process two or three times and it always lifted our mood and put smiles on our faces. (Note: I cannot carry a tune in a bucket so the smiles could have been from my horrible singing, but who cares? We were smiling!)

Replace your negatives with something to read, watch, listen to, write, or think about and your mood will lift and improve in minutes.

Breaking the Brain Chain

One of the biggest helpers in relieving anxiety is to break your thought patterns. You can do this in several ways:

- Count your breaths. You can breathe in to the count of 4 or 5 and out to the same count of 4 or 5.
- You can watch a kaleidoscope spin around, something flying in the air, a fidget spinner twirl, or you can even follow your fingers as they move in an up and down and side to side pattern, as I instructed my daughter's coach to do previously.
- You can skip count by any number. This is my personal favorite. If my anxiety was low, I would skip count by 3 or 4's (3, 6, 9, 12, 15, 18, etc.) If my anxiety was high, I would skip count by something harder for me like 7's or 8's. If my anxiety was off-the-chain high, I would skip count backwards.

Any of these suggestions will break the chain of your thoughts and reverse anxiety simply because the mind can't think two thoughts at the same time. If you are figuring out what 7 times 7 is, you can't be thinking about "what if" your anxiety goes higher.

Daily Doses of Dedication

One of the best tools that helped me recover from anxiety was journaling. I would write this at the top of every page:

Today is a new day!
You get a fresh start each and every day!
So make the most of today.

I also included these parts in my journal,

- My goals for how I wanted to think and feel for the day
- My plans for the day
- My big fear for the day
- My little fear for the day
- Where I thought either of the above came from
- My morning Positive Point
- My victory for the day
- The techniques I successfully used the day before
- How I could improve any technique
- My success in how well I succeeded in my goals and plans for the day.

One of the first things that journaling brought to my attention was that I had to stop letting the smallest thing ruin my whole entire day. If I was feeling stressed, I asked myself: Will this matter in a year from now? If yes, then I did something about it. If no, then I stopped letting it bother me.

The smallest thing can ruin your whole entire day, but only if you let it. Stop letting it.

Journaling also showed me that my anxiety would go up if I was bored. I used this knowledge to begin teaching myself new hobbies. I learned how to cross stitch, crochet, and scrapbook to entertain myself. These are still hobbies that I enjoy today, when I am not out riding my motorcycle, of course.

Smell the Calm

This is a technique that I still use all the time. Find scents that remind you of something happy. I have used flower oils, candles, sachets, and even a gum eraser. These scents soothe me and make my heart happy. It is also fun to shop for these things with my daughter. We always have a good time candle shopping. Some of my favorite scents are,

- Honeysuckle
- Eucalyptus with mint
- Sage
- Pumpkin spice
- Beach smells
- Fall scents
- Pine
- Clove
- Sugar cookie
- Lavender

Learn to Love You

In closing, the best advice I can share to help you with your anxiety would be to learn to love you.

"You is smart, you is kind, you is important!"

We too often joke while using this movie quote from The Help when we need to be writing it on our bathroom mirrors, with large dry erase markers, using correct grammar, of course.

Then we need to forget all the drama and let go of all the grudges we've been holding inside. Forgive yourself for any you created and forgive others, not because they deserve it, but because you deserve peace.

Let yourself finally be happy for once, not because you've earned it, simply because you deserve it.

Finally, don't blame yourself for where you are in life. You have done the best you knew how to do. As you learn better, you will do better. I can remember way back when I first began learning how to train my brain. I honestly thought it would be a one and done event. Little did I know then that this would be a lifelong journey. And what a journey it has been.

CHAPTER 11

BONUS MONSTER TRAINING SCRIPTS

◇◇◇◇

You can reword to create Monster Training Scripts for any occasion. I have created them for specific events from tests to medical procedures. For better results, record them and follow your instructions in your own voice. After all, it was our own voices who created the monster, so what better way to train it then use our own voice? Below are some examples of the ones I use.

FOR HEALING

1. Sit or lay in a comfortable position.
2. Focus on your feet and take a slow and controlled deep breath in that fills your belly. As you focus on your feet, mentally say, "All disease is leaving this area. This area is now healthy and filled with light." Picture this area flowing with a soft white light.
3. Focus on your lower legs from right above your knees on down and take a slow and controlled deep breath in that fills your belly. As you focus on this area, mentally say, "All disease is leaving this area. This

area is now healthy and filled with light." Picture this area flowing with a soft white light.

4. Focus on your thigh muscles and take a slow and controlled deep breath in that fills your belly. As you focus on this area, mentally say, "All disease is leaving this area. This area is now healthy and filled with light." Picture this area flowing with a soft white light.

5. Focus on the area from your belly button down to the top of your thighs and take a slow and controlled deep breath in that fills your belly. As you focus on this area, mentally say, "All disease is leaving this area. This area is now healthy and filled with light." Picture this area flowing with a soft white light.

6. Focus on your back from the base of your neck to the top of your hips and take a slow and controlled deep breath in that fills your belly. As you focus on this area, mentally say, "All disease is leaving this area. This area is now healthy and filled with light." Picture this area flowing with a soft white light.

7. Focus on your front from the top of your shoulders to the bottom of your belly and take a slow and controlled deep breath in that fills your belly. As you focus on this area, mentally say, "All disease is leaving this area. This area is now healthy and filled with light." Picture this area flowing with a soft white light.

8. Focus on your neck paying special attention to the back of your neck. We tend to hold much of our stress and anxiety here and take a slow and controlled deep breath in that fills your belly. As you focus on this area, mentally say, "All disease is leaving this area.

This area is now healthy and filled with light." Picture this area flowing with a soft white light.

9. Focus on the back of your head, all the way up and over the top of your head to your hairline. Take a slow and controlled deep breath in that fills your belly. As you focus on this area, mentally say, "All disease is leaving this area. This area is now healthy and filled with light." Picture this area flowing with a soft white light.

10. Focus on your face, paying special attention to your forehead and jaw. Take a slow and controlled deep breath in that fills your belly. As you focus on this area, mentally say, "All disease is leaving this area. This area is now healthy and filled with light." Picture this area flowing with a soft white light.

11. Focus on your eyes and the tiny muscles surrounding your eyes. Take a slow and controlled deep breath in that fills your belly. As you focus on this area, mentally say, "All disease is leaving this area. This area is now healthy and filled with light." Picture this area flowing with a soft white light.

Now you are in the alpha state or close enough to it.

Next, focus on how you physically want to feel. If one part of your body hurts, focus on a part that does not, and imagine your whole body feeling like the unaffected part. For instance, I had a shoulder injury so I would focus on how the healthy shoulder felt and imaging the injured shoulder feeling the same way. Focus fully and intently on the healthy area.

Visualize health flooding your entire body. Picture how healthy you look and what you could or would be doing as you enjoy this perfect health. Imagine the calm and thankful look on your face as your pain leaves you completely.

After you have done this, tell yourself mentally that when you count to five, you will feel wide awake and perfectly healthy.

Stay in this state for as long as you feel productive in it, then count to five and open your eyes and stretch, or yawn, or do whatever feels natural to you.

FOR IMPROVING MINDSETS

1. Sit or lay in a comfortable position.
2. Take 10 deep breaths in and out, counting backwards mentally from 10 to 1.
3. Imagine a zipper on your forehead, at your hairline. If you are bald, imagine it where your hairline would be. Imagine yourself reaching up and unzipping the zipper.
4. Picture a stream of bright yellow liquid coming down from the heavens, through your roof, through the ceiling, and entering into the zipper opening.
5. Imagine this yellow light flowing through your body to its lowest point. Imagine it then beginning to fill your body, slowly and steadily. The last part of your body to be filled will be the top of your head where the zipper is. Once full, imagine yourself zipping the zipper closed.
6. Tell yourself, "This yellow liquid is magical. It will pull all negativity from my body and mind when prompted by each negative word."
7. Pick any or all of the following negative emotions that you want to work on. Say each of the following words as you take a breath in and let it out. Notice how the yellow liquid loses it brightness and becomes dingy and dirty as you say each word and pull the corresponding negativity out of your body.

a. Fear – All thoughts and feelings of fear are now being pulled from your mind and body and being absorbed into the yellow liquid.

b. Stress - All thoughts and feelings of stress are now being pulled from your mind and body and being absorbed into the yellow liquid.

c. Negativity - All thoughts and feelings of negativity are now being pulled from your mind and body and being absorbed into the yellow liquid.

d. Disease - All thoughts and feelings of disease are now being pulled from your mind and body and being absorbed into the yellow liquid.

e. Jealousy- All thoughts and feelings of jealousy towards others or other's situations are now being pulled from your mind and body and being absorbed into the yellow liquid.

f. Judgement - All thoughts and feelings of judgements toward others are now being pulled from your mind and body and being absorbed into the yellow liquid.

g. Hatred - All thoughts and feelings of hatred towards others are now being pulled from your mind and body and being absorbed into the yellow liquid.

h. Any other negative emotion you wish to work on.

8. Now notice how dingy and dirty the yellow liquid is.

9. Imagine that your feet are valves, and that your heels are the opening. Mentally open the valves and feel the

dingy and dirty yellow liquid flow out of your body. Notice how light, refreshed and positive you feel as it does so.

10. Picture the valves closing once all the yellow liquid is gone.

11. Mentally tell yourself that your mind and body are now reset to positive settings. You mind will be clearer. Your mood will be lighter. You will begin to notice all of the positive things around you. You will see yourself in a more loving and more positive manner.

12. Enjoy this safe and happy place that you have created.

13. When you are ready, count to five, and tell yourself you are awake and alert, and ready to enjoy your day.

FOR HELP IN SPECIFIC SITUATIONS OR EVENTS

If possible, do this for several days before the event.

1. Sit or lay back in a comfortable position.

2. Countdown from 25 to 1, taking in and letting out a deep breath with each number.

3. After you reach 1, imagine yourself getting ready for the situation or the event. Picture yourself feeling calm and relaxed.

4. Next, imagine you are in the situation or at the event. Imagine how you want to look. Visualize the expressions on your face. Do this in as much detail as you can.

5. Then, imagine the event is over. Feel how happy you are with how you felt and how you looked. Feel how

proud you are of controlling your thoughts and your feelings.

6.   Finally, allow yourself to slowly come back to reality, but do so knowing that you are carrying the positive thoughts and feelings with you as your energy goes before you preparing the situation or event to be as you imagined, or even better.

CHAPTER 12

RECOMMENDED READS

◇◇◇

Anxiety & Panic Attacks *by Robert Handly*

You Can Heal Your Life *by Louise Hay*

When Bad Things Happen to Good
People *by Harold S. Kushner*

Battlefield of the Mind *by Joyce Meyer (Christian)*

The Body Never Lies *by Alice Miller*

The Body Keeps the Score by *Bessel Van Der Kolk, MD*

The Silva Method *by Jose Silva*

Boundaries by *Dr. Henry Cloud*

While not a book, I also use various Self Hypnosis and Subliminal recordings from www.potentialsunlimited. These can easily be downloaded to your phone.

ACKNOWLEDGEMENTS

◇◇◇◇

First and foremost, thank you God, who makes all things possible. Thank you for blessing me with the gift of storytelling. Thank you for sending me each and every person who helped make this dream a reality. Most of all, thank you for your unconditional love. You are eternal. You are limitless! You are my God!

It takes so much more than creativity, time, and effort for an author to write a book. It takes a tribe to help them finish it and to get it published.

My tribe starts with my family.

Thank you to my wonderful husband, Dwight, and our two amazing kiddos, Austin and Makenna. Thank you first for pushing me to pursue my dreams. I could not do what I do without your support and encouragement. Thank you also for cooking, cleaning, and keeping the house running so that I could get another thousand words in for the day. Thank you for understanding when I just needed to write for 5 more minutes and for forgiving me when that 5 minutes lasts for over an hour. You are my heart.

Thank you to my aunt, Carole Marcella-Fair! You are my cheerleader and proofreader all in one. Thank you for our day-cations when you help me get away from the computer so that I can destress and recharge when I need to. You always help me keep my feet on solid ground and remind me about what is important.

Thank you to my aunt, Gayle Gray! You taught me about plant therapy and have encouraged my green thumb for longer than I can remember. You have always had my back, my front, and everything in between.

Thank you, Jessica Thatcher! You are my soul sister and confidante. You lift me up when I am down and give me a kick in the pants when it's warranted. You make sure what I wanted to say gets said and said correctly.

Thank you, Audrey Goodman! You help me keep it real for those that this book is really for. Your insight and input mean as much to me as your friendship.

Thank you, Billy Sticker! You lead by example! You have inspired me to work harder, stretch myself further, and create better. Thank you for all your technical help and help on pulling it all together.

Thank you, Chasity Parsons! Thank you for introducing me to Wind Therapy! Thank you for becoming so much more than a friend, you are my ride or die bestie!

Thank you, Nancy Gandy! You inspire me to write and keep writing whatever makes my heart happy. You have taught me to live my dream by living yours so well.

This book could not have been written without my parents.

Thank you, Saundra Whittington for raising me to be independent and to think for myself.

Thank you, Scooter Jackson! You taught me by example how to see the story in anything and how to make it interesting for others.

Together, you taught me what kind of person I wanted to be, and I wouldn't be half the person I am if it had not been for you.

Lastly, a few special people who help complete my world and add to the reason that I smile, Michael & Kristen Gandy, Bryce & Sydney Coble, James D. Bottley, and Reagan Matthews.

I love each and every one of you listed above.
You are so special to me!
You make my heart happy and life worth living!

ABOUT THE AUTHOR

A native of Kountze, Texas, Author, Rebell R. Wade is a retired certified elementary school teacher. She lives on the family farm with her husband, Dwight, and her two children, Austin and Makenna, along with a zoo of chickens, rabbits, pigs, cows, and dogs.

Rebell finds joy in being outdoors, reading, gardening, tending the farm, and riding her motorcycle. Her passion is helping others live their best lives possible whether it is through education, mental, physical, emotional, or in a financial capacity.

www.ingramcontent.com/pod-product-compliance
Lightning Source LLC
Chambersburg PA
CBHW061153040426

42445CB00013B/1675

* 9 7 8 0 5 7 8 7 9 6 6 8 0 *